I0176913

SIMPLE STRATEGIES FOR

STRESS RELIEF

How to Reduce Anxiety, Regain Control of
Your Life, and Beat Stress the Easy Way

Nathalie Thompson

© 2016 Nathalie Thompson. All rights reserved.

No part of this publication may be reproduced, stored in a retrieval system, or transmitted in any form or by any means – electronic, mechanical, photocopying, recording, scanning, or otherwise – except for brief quotations in critical reviews or articles, without the prior written permission of the author.

The author of this book does not dispense medical advice or prescribe the use of any technique as a form of treatment for physical, emotional, or medical problems without the advice of a licensed physician, either directly or indirectly. Any use of information in this book is at the reader's discretion and risk. The advice and strategies contained herein may not be suitable for your particular situation, and you should always consult with a professional where appropriate. Neither the author nor the publisher shall be liable for any loss, claim, or damage resulting from the use or misuse of the suggestions made.

All trademarks and registered trademarks appearing in this book are the property of their respective owners.

For information visit the author's web sites at:

www.NathalieThompson.com
www.VibeShifting.com

ISBN: 978-0-9948844-3-5 (ebk)
ISBN: 978-0-9948844-9-7 (pbk)

Table of Contents

Introduction

"IF THE PROBLEM CAN BE SOLVED WHY WORRY?
IF THE PROBLEM CANNOT BE SOLVED,
WORRYING WILL DO YOU NO GOOD."
~ŚĀNTIDEVA

A Google search will tell you that stress is "a state of mental or emotional strain or tension resulting from adverse or very demanding circumstances".[1] It's an interesting definition because it doesn't attempt to clarify what "adverse" or "demanding" actually entail.

In other words, it means that stress is a very subjective thing. No two people will interpret a situation in the same way, so no two people will respond to a situation in the same way. What is considered stressful for one person, therefore, may not be considered stressful by another.

What makes a situation stressful for us is *how we feel about it and react to it.* And therein lies the secret to overcoming our stress: if it's our *interpretation* of the situations and events in our lives, and our reactions to those interpretations, that causes us to feel stressed then learning how to manage and dissolve that stress begins with understanding our unique stressors and stress responses. *Simple Strategies for Stress Relief* is designed to help you do just that.

Why "Quick Fixes" for Stress Don't Work

Stress has become a trendy issue in our modern on-the-go world, and everyone out there seems to have a specialty course designed to fix your stress-inducing problems for you. Everywhere you look it seems there are new stress reduction retreats or "Stress Management Bootcamps" popping up like mushrooms after a rainstorm. I've never tried any of these myself, so I can't tell you whether they work or not, but in my opinion, anything that has "bootcamp" in the title is more likely to add to my stress level rather than decrease it!

All cynicism aside, the biggest problem with all of these fancy relaxation retreats and rapid-fire bootcamp approaches is that eventually they come to an end and you're right back where you started. Your regular life has been patiently waiting for you, and all the things that stress you out are still there, unchanged and as potent as ever. On top of that, every last one of these programs is based on the idea that you can turn your entire life around in "just ten days" or with whatever miracle "cure" happens to be offered.

But the truth is that there is no quick-fix to stress. Stress is a mindset and behavioural issue; it's a result of habits that you've formed over time in your thinking and in your doing. You can't reprogram those ingrained habits in "ten days or less", and no fixed-length intensive system, no matter who created it, is going to magically cure you of your stress. That's just not how it works.

It's About Creating New Habits

"But wait a minute!" you're saying, "The title of *this* book is *Simple Strategies for Stress Relief*! How is that any different from all those other programs out there?!" Good question. I said that there is no magic bullet cure for stress, and there isn't. But that doesn't mean that getting your stress level under control and finding the balance you so desperately want in life has to be hard.

You *can*, in fact, regain control of your life and beat stress, and you can do it easily, using simple, easy-to-implement techniques that you can use whenever you need them. Any one of the Stress Buster techniques I talk about in this book, for example, will help you to achieve quick, *but temporary*, stress relief, usually within minutes of using it.

Temporary stress relief is not why I wrote this book, though. It's not what I want for you, and it's not what you want for yourself. If you picked this book up, I'm betting it's because you're looking for a long-term solution, with long-lasting results. And that's what *Simple Strategies for Stress Relief* is really about: real, lasting solutions. It's about creating the building blocks that will help you to reduce your stress and anxiety levels for good.

There is, however, one catch: achieving long-lasting results, in *any* area of your life, takes some amount of effort. It is going to take dedication on your part to get the results you really want, and if you're serious about stress reduction, you're going to have to make some changes in the way you *do* things and in the way you *think* about things.

If you really want to change things and live a more relaxed and stress-free life, it starts with your mindset, and with the little things that you do on a daily basis that all perpetuate that vicious cycle of anxiety and stress.

How to Use This Book

Now, at this point you may be feeling nervous about this whole thing – changing your thought patterns and changing your habits sounds like a lot of hard work! Don't panic. I promised you a guide on how to beat stress the easy way, and that's what you're going to get.

This is a book about easy, yet practical, real-world techniques for identifying and coping with stress *in the long-term*. It's about transforming the way you react to situations so that they no longer have the power to bring you down. There are two ways in which you can use this book to do just that:

For instant relief:

You can skip ahead to Chapters 5, 6, 7 and 8 and use any technique that appeals to you on its own for almost instant (but temporary) relief in specific situations that are causing you to feel anxious, worried, or stressed.

Most of the techniques and strategies in this book are quick enough that you can use them and start seeing results in just a few minutes. Some of them do take longer than that to implement, but I promise they're worth the effort.

For long-term, lasting change:

Make the decision to do something that impacts the rest of your life, and go through the whole book from the beginning. In Chapter 1, I talk about what stress is and what the effects of it are if left unchecked. This is going to help you to understand why you're doing these exercises and it will give you a reason to keep at it as you start making the changes in your life that will help you to keep stress in check.

In Chapter 2, I explain my views on what the *real* causes of stress are, so that you have a better understanding of the kind of power you already have within you to make those changes you want in your life.

In Chapter 3, I walk you through my "Four-Step Stress Reduction Process" where you're going to gain some important insight into your own unique stress responses, and learn to identify your specific stress triggers and current coping techniques.

With this information, you're then going to build a custom stress reduction plan by picking and choosing the strategies and techniques from Chapters 5 through 8 that most appeal to you and your specific situation.

Regardless of which approach you use (instant or long-term), with all of the Stress Buster strategies I discuss in this book, you'll get increasingly better results the more often you use them. Consistency is the key to creating new habits, and as the techniques you choose become more familiar you'll find that you start using them automatically, without even having to think about it, whenever you're in a stressful situation. You'll also notice that the more you use the techniques, the faster you start noticing stress-reduction results.

There's one final note before we get started: one of the techniques that I talk about in Chapter 6 is meditation. People are often confused about how to start meditating and they're never sure they're "doing it right". If you struggle with this same issue, I've created a bonus ten minute guided audio meditation to help you get started. You can pick up your free copy of this MP3 file at:

http://www.nathaliethompson.com/stress-relief-meditation/

PART I: UNDERSTANDING YOUR STRESS

Chapter 1
Feeling Stressed?

"SOME PEOPLE ARE SO USED TO EXPERIENCING STRESS
THAT THEY DON'T REMEMBER
WHAT LIFE WAS LIKE WITHOUT IT."
~ANDREW BERNSTEIN

If you're feeling the need for some good stress-busting strategies in your life, you're not alone. In a 2014 report released by the American Psychological Association, 75% of American adults reported feeling at least one symptom of stress in the previous month.[2] That same report also found that 51% of women and 32% of men have lain awake at night, unable to sleep because of stress. Interestingly enough, however, 20% of survey respondents also stated that they had never even tried to relieve or manage their stress.

For many people stress has become the standard mode of operation. In this plugged-in, constantly connected, and always-on-the-go world of ours, it's almost as if we've given up on the idea that life could be anything *other* than stressful, and just accepted it as par-for-course for adults everywhere.

We really can't avoid being exposed to stress-inducing situations, and as a result, our systems are always on high alert, ready to fight or flee at a moment's notice. But there's nothing there to fight or flee from, and all of those stress hormones that are only designed to be in our bodies for short periods of time before being burned up through action are left coursing through our systems for far too long.

The problem with all of this constant stress is that it has such a detrimental effect on both our mental and physical health.[3] Long-term stress can lead to physical symptoms such as: recurring headaches, high blood-pressure, stomach pains and insomnia, and can also reduce your body's ability to fight off colds. Psychologically, stress can cause decreased productivity, anxiety, irritability and depression.

The Old School Response

Sounds like a disaster in the making, doesn't it? What's a person to do in the face of this onslaught of awfulness? The response of modern medicine to all of

these stress-related illnesses is to prescribe drugs. Drugs for blood pressure, drugs for anxiety, drugs for insomnia, drugs for depression, and drugs to treat the side-effects of other drugs and counter-balance the way they interact with each other.

Now, I'm not saying that you should not *start* taking particular medications, or that you should *stop* taking any medications that you are currently on (that is a decision that should only be made in conjunction with, and under the care of, a licensed health care practitioner). I do feel, however, that in many cases, the use of drugs is a bandaid solution that focuses solely on the symptoms and doesn't deal with the real cause of the problem. And when you only treat the symptoms, you're not really fixing anything.

If you want to get rid of a dandelion, for example, you don't just chop the leaves off or it will grow right back in just a few days; if you want a permanent solution, you have to go to the root and pull out the entire weed.

In my opinion, this is the only way to deal with problem of stress: by finding effective coping strategies that not only allow us to find temporary relief from the stress *symptoms*, but that also address the root *causes* and permanently reduce our stress-levels over the long-term.

Fortunately, it is indeed possible to learn how to effectively cope with stress, reduce your tension levels and increase your feelings of relaxation and peacefulness. It starts with accepting the fact that you are in control of your life and circumstances, and by using that power to make positive changes for yourself and your own mental and physical health. It starts with making changes to your *mindset*; the way that you think about the world and your experience in it.

Chapter 2:
What Causes Stress?

*"THE PROBLEM IS NOT THE PROBLEM.
THE PROBLEM IS YOUR ATTITUDE
ABOUT THE PROBLEM."*
~CAPT. JACK SPARROW
(FROM THE MOVIE 'PIRATES OF THE CARIBBEAN')

If you search the phrase "causes of stress" on Google, you will get over 94 million results. It's fascinating; page after page of search results talking about family problems, health issues, job-related situations, financial concerns, etc. show up in the search results as leading causes of stress in the modern world.

The really interesting thing about all of these search results, though, is that they are all wrong; none of these things are the *cause* of your stress. No situation, no matter how bad it is, can *cause* stress without your consent. What causes stress is your *thoughts* – your *reaction to* and *interpretation of* the situation at hand. In other words, stress begins in your mind, and if you want to learn how to control your stress, that's where you have to begin.

Your own mind can be your worst enemy or your most powerful ally. It all depends on how you choose to use it. Learn to control your thoughts and you can change your entire world; in the words of Wayne Dyer: "when you change the way you look at things, the things you look at change". If you change the way you think about the situations that stress you out, you automatically change the effect they have you. At the heart of it all, it really is that simple. It only gets complicated when we bounce around wildly from situation to situation, focused so completely on everything that's going wrong in our lives, that we forget the fact that no difficulty is insurmountable and no storm lasts forever.

Most people career through their lives on auto-pilot, constantly in reaction mode to the things that happen around them. But in order to effectively deal with stress, you need to stop blindly *reacting* to the events of your life, and start deliberately *responding* to them instead.

It seems like such a minor difference, reaction versus response, but it is a critical one. If you really want to put an end to the stress in your life, then *you* are the one who must deliberately make the decision to *want* that change, and then deliberately take the action necessary to make it happen. You will always have situations in your life that have the potential to cause stress, but you alone have the power to decide whether those situations are going to control you or whether *you* are the one who will remain in control.

Four Steps to Relieve Stress

Reaction versus response; it really is up to you. And with that in mind, I'm going to share a four-step process that will help you to deal more effectively with the stress in your life by helping you to understand:

- what it is that causes you to experience stress;
- how you, specifically, react when these things happen; and
- what you can do to change the way it all affects you.

This process is going to help you make that shift from reacting to responding to your life stressors so that you can finally make those lasting changes you've been seeking. We're going to go over the entire process in detail in the next chapter, but for now, here's the overview:

Step 1: Recognize your own stress response.

The first step in dealing with stress in to recognize *when* you are experiencing symptoms of stress and *what* those specific reactions are (because your stress responses are not necessarily going to be the same as someone else's).

Step 2: Identify your unique stressors.

The second step is to figure out what is *really* causing your stress. What are the specific triggers that are most likely to set off your stress response?

Step 3: Understand how you currently cope with stress and how it's affecting your life.

If you want to make a change and improve your ability to cope with stress, you need to be aware of what you're currently doing when stress hits you and whether it's getting you the kind of results you want.

Step 4: Create your action plan.

If your current coping mechanisms aren't working for you, then it's time to find some new ones that will!

And that's all it takes to get yourself started and on your way to a more relaxed and peaceful life; just four simple steps! Sounds easy-peasy, doesn't it? That's because it is! Big changes don't have to be hard, but they do have to start with a *choice*. This is where real change begins; this is where you start taking control of your life and how you choose to live it; this is where it all starts. It's *your* decision. So shall we get started? Good. Let's go...

Chapter 3:
The Four-Step Stress Reduction Process

"Getting stress out of your life takes more than prayer alone. You must take action to make changes and stop doing whatever is causing the stress. You can learn to calm down in the way you handle things."
~Joyce Meyer

The "Four-Step Stress Reduction Process" is the key to effective, long-term stress reduction, and it involves a certain amount of introspection and self-awareness; if you really want to get a handle on your stress levels, you have to start by understanding your own unique stressors and stress responses. Again, the really odd thing about stress is how personal it is; no two people will have exactly the same response to a situation they both perceive as "stressful", and no two people will ever interpret a situation in exactly the same way either.

A situation that one person might find intolerably stressful might be a minor annoyance, or even a complete non-issue to another. (For example, when I find large spiders crawling around inside my house, I get seriously freaked out, but my son just thinks they're "cool" and wants to play with them.) It's all a matter of perception and perspective.

And that's why this process is so important; it allows you to really look within and understand how you react to your life experiences. Only by understanding yourself in this way will you be able to make lasting changes and regain control of your life. It's about learning how to *stop* being a passive reactor to the events of your life and *start* taking charge of how you respond to and interpret things so that you can create the kind of life experience you *want* to have.

Step 1: Recognize Your Unique Stress Response

I mentioned in Chapter 1 that when we are exposed to a situation that induces stress, our bodies react with a "fight or flight" mechanism, boosting our adrenaline levels and getting us ready for action. This was helpful in the days when stress meant you needed to either fight or outrun the sabre-tooth tiger that just appeared in your camp, but in modern society there are not a lot of situations that call for that kind of desperate, intense physical action. All of that extra energy, therefor, stays pent-up in our bodies and shows up as symptoms like pain, tension and anxiety. It's as if all the energy that would have been spent either fighting or outrunning the danger is turned inwards and quietly unleashed on your own body.

Everybody reacts to this adrenaline-induced onslaught differently, however, and the first key to learning how to manage stress is to understand how your own body manifests this internal energy surge. Your body is a precision instrument designed to give you constant feedback about what is happening within; all you have to do is learn how to interpret its signals and pay attention to what it's telling you. If something is wrong, your body will tell you before things get critical. It's like all those gauges on your car's dashboard; they're there for a reason, and you ignore their warnings at your own risk!

Close your eyes for a moment and just listen to your body. Do you feel any tension or soreness in your joints, tendons or muscles? Do you often feel like you're on the edge of a headache? Is your jaw clenched? Are you frowning? Are your hands balled up or clenched?

Does your stomach feel "off"? Is your breathing rapid or shallow?

All of these physical symptoms can come from being under a constant state of stress. For the next few days, make it a point to really start paying attention to your body and how it feels; make a note of any physical symptoms you experience that tell you how your own body is showing stress.

Step 2: Identify Your Unique Stressors

The next step of the process involve figuring out the actual causes of your personal stress response, and one of the best tools for determining what your true stressors are is a stress journal.

Find a little notebook, or just staple some sheets of paper together, and start a daily journal or log book in which you record and analyse the situations that stress you during the day.

When you feel stressed, write it down. Make a note of what happened that triggered the stressful feelings. How did the situation make you feel? Note your emotions and your physical sensations. When adding to your log book, ask yourself:

1. What happened that made me feel stressed?
2. How did it make me feel (physical and emotional symptoms)?

3. How did I react to the situation? (What did I do when I felt the stress?)
4. What did I do to make myself feel better, if anything?

After you've been using your log book for a few days, you will likely start to notice patterns developing that will give you valuable information about the types of situations and experiences that cause your stress levels to rise. For instance, you may notice that whenever there's a pile of dishes in the kitchen sink, you get upset, or whenever you're stuck in traffic you get angry.

What recurring themes do you notice when you look through your log book? Do you tend to get stressed at certain times of the day, in particular types of situations, or around specific people? Make a note of any patterns that you can see.

Real versus Assumed Stressors

Oftentimes, what we *think* causes our stress and what *actually* causes our stress are two very different things! For example, is it the crumbs on the floor that really leaves you stressed, or is it that those crumbs make you feel that no one seems to help out around the house? Is it the fact that you and your family have so many scheduled activities that makes you stressed, or is it the fact that you feel you're not organized enough to deal with it effectively that is the real cause?

Most of the stress we experience in life is actually triggered by particular *thoughts or feelings* that we have about a particular situation, rather than by the situation itself.

Take a look at your log book, and the patterns you've identified. Within those patterns, determine where the real stressor lies. Once you understand what the real trigger for your stress response is, you can take steps to deal with it effectively.

Step 3: Your Current Coping Strategies

One of the most important things you need to understand in order to regain control of your life is that no one can take away your stress except you. You need to accept responsibility for your own well-being. This is not blaming you for being stressed, this is helping you to understand where the real power lies: *with you.*

When we assume that someone else's action or inaction affects our stress levels (for example, "If Jane would just help out more, I wouldn't be so stressed!"), we give away our power. This is the path that leads to depression and other mental health issues, so *don't give away your power*! Accept responsibility for your own moods and mental and physical health; reclaim your power and decide right now to create the kind of life you want to live.

Once you have identified your unique stressors, the next step in engineering long-term stress reduction is to analyse your current coping strategies. How do you currently cope with stress? Do you primarily use strategies designed for temporary escape from your problems, or do you use strategies that help you build functional coping skills and increase your resiliency in the face of life's normal ups and downs?

Escape-Based Coping Strategies

Escape-based coping strategies are just what they sound like: strategies that allow us to escape from our feelings of stress and anxiety. On the surface, these types of strategies often seem quicker and less work to implement, and they may even feel like they're helping in the short-term, but in the long run they just compound the problem and make things worse. They're just more of those bandaid solutions I talked about in Chapter 1 that cover things up without actually fixing them. And the thing with escapes is that sooner or later what you're running away from always catches up with you.

Here are some examples of common escape-based strategies. Take a look at the list below and make a note of any strategies that you currently use to deal with your stress levels:

- Smoking

27

- Self-medicating with drugs or alcohol
- Using prescription drugs to help you relax or sleep
- Overscheduling yourself to avoid thinking about things
- Lashing out at others with either words or physical violence
- Eating too much or too little
- Avoiding life by watching too much TV

If you are aware of any other strategies you use that do not help to improve your mental or physical health, note them, too.

Most people will use at least one of these escape-based strategies at some time or other, but if you find yourself using a lot of them, or resorting to them often, then it's definitely time to re-evaluate your coping mechanisms and come up with healthier alternatives.

Functional Coping Strategies

On the flip side of escape-based coping strategies for stress are the functional strategies. A functional coping strategy is one that benefits you in the long run; these types of strategies help to increase your emotional and physical health and provide you with lasting solutions and mechanisms for coping with stress. They increase your ability to weather the inevitable stormy periods in life.

If you use any functional coping strategies in your life, make a note of them, and ask yourself how well they have been working for you. If any of your functional strategies have provided even moderate relief from your stress in the past, and if you have found enjoyment in any of them, then they can provide a foundation that you can build on in the next step.

Step 4: Create Your Action Plan

Now that you've done the crucial self-assessment steps and figured out your own particular stress triggers, responses and current coping mechanisms, it's time to move onto the final stage of the "Four-Step-Stress Reduction Process", and that is to create an action plan for how you're actually going to deal with your stress from here on in. In order to create your plan, you're going to be choosing specific coping strategies from the next few chapters to use whenever you start to feel stressed.

My Stress Buster Strategies are a plug-and-play menu of healthy ways to deal with stress. They're like building blocks that you can stack together and use in different configurations to create a truly personalized blueprint for reducing both your stress reactions to specific situations *and* your overall, baseline stress level, too. I've categorized these Stress Busters as physical, psychological, environmental, or social strategies, depending on what they involve:

- **Physical Stress Busters** are those which involve physical activity or changes;
- **Psychological Stress Busters** involve defined changes to the way in which you think about and interpret things;
- **Environmental Stress Busters** involve changes to the space around you; and
- **Social Stress Busters** involve your interactions with other people

In the next four chapters we'll be taking a closer look at each of these categories, and I'll be giving you lots of specific, easy-to-implement techniques within each category that you can add to your action plan and start using right away for quick stress-relief results!

Depending on your personality and the unique stressors that you identified in step 2 of the "Four-Step Stress Reduction Process", some of the techniques will be more effective for you than others. Also, what works for you in one situation may not work in another, so feel free to mix-and-match and use different strategies at different times.

PART 2:
STRESS BUSTER
STRATEGIES

Chapter 4:
What Are Stress Buster Strategies?

"THE GREATEST WEAPON AGAINST STRESS IS OUR ABILITY TO CHOOSE ONE THOUGHT OVER ANOTHER."
~ WILLIAM JAMES

So this is the moment you've been waiting for: the super-list of Stress Buster Strategies! These are the functional, healthy coping strategies that you're going to use to create your personal stress-relief action plan.

Here's how it works: in the next four chapters, you're going to get specific techniques for alleviating stress, grouped into each of the four different types of functional coping strategies: physical stress busters, psychological stress busters, environmental stress busters, and social stress busters.

Before you try any of these strategies, however, I want you to get yourself a notebook (or several pieces of paper) and a pen, and your log from Chapter 3. For each of the patterns that you identified in your log, use a new page and write the trigger at the top of the page (e.g "traffic jams" or "work situation").

Now, as you read through the different types of strategies and techniques, make a note of any specific Stress Busters that appeal to you and which you think would be useful in the particular situation that you noted at the top of each of your pages. These are your action plans for your specific stress triggers.

Keep your action plans handy for easy reference over the next few days and weeks; eventually the Stress Busters that you use most and which are most effective for you will become a habit and you won't need your plans anymore; you will have finally made that mindset shift that leads to a less stressed, and more balanced and peaceful life!

Chapter 5:
Physical Stress Busters

*"IF YOU ASKED ME WHAT THE SINGLE MOST IMPORTANT
KEY TO LONGEVITY IS, I WOULD HAVE TO SAY IT IS
AVOIDING WORRY, STRESS AND TENSION."*
~GEORGE BURNS

Physical coping strategies involve action; they involve changes to the way in which you move or the way you treat your body. These strategies often seem counter-intuitive, in the sense that it's not always easy to see the connection between the strategy and how it affects your stress levels, but I've tried to provide a short explanation of the "why" behind each technique to help you better understand how it works.

1. Adjust your posture.

When we feel stressed, we often slump over and hunch our shoulders forward as if we're carrying the weight of all that stress right on them. This increases the tension in our shoulder muscles, neck, back and chest and just adds to the feeling of stress!

Try straightening up: put your shoulders back, lift your chin and lengthen your spine. Proper posture eases muscle tension and helps to reduce the physical strain of stress.

2. Do some stretches.

By the end of the day, most of us can feel the tension in our muscles. We're tense from the day's events, and stress actually makes this feeling worse, adding soreness and strain to the general tension. Doing some gentle stretches at regular intervals throughout the day can help alleviate this build-up of tension.

Something as simple as rolling your shoulders, tilting your head from side-to-side and stretching out your forearms by putting your hands in an upside-down prayer position can work wonders to relieve bunched up muscles and tendons and get your blood flowing again.

3. Take a walk.

Taking a short walking break from what you're doing can make a world of difference in your stress levels. Not only do you get a change of scenery, but you get moving, which increases your circulation and wakes you up.

If you can, leave your desk and head outside at lunch time for a mid-day walk and enjoy the sunshine for an added bonus. If you really can't get away, then taking even just a few minutes to walk around your office floor or down to the coffee shop in the lobby can be really helpful.

4. Just breathe.

When we're stressed, our breathing often becomes shallow and rapid which just amplifies the feelings of panic and distress we may be feeling. Taking a few minutes to breathe deeply and slowly can do wonders for slowing down your heart rate and inducing a feeling of tranquility.

Close your eyes and take a deep breath in, letting it fill your abdomen up like a balloon. Hold that breath for a second or two, and then slowly let it out. Repeat this sequence three to five times to help you feel more relaxed.

5. Smile!

This sounds oh-so-simplistic, but it's such a powerful tool. You smile automatically when you feel happy, but did you know that smiling when you don't feel happy can actually improve your mood and make you feel more relaxed?

If you consciously try and make yourself smile when you are feeling stressed, it really does make you feel better.

6. Work it out.

Regular physical exercise is a great way to release tension and stress. Take a walk in the sunshine, or head to the gym and spend some time on the treadmill. Go to a yoga class or try out tae-boxing or Zumba for something fun and different. The key is to find an activity that you really enjoy doing – something that you will actually look forward to.

And if you're not a treadmill or gym type of person, then put on your favourite happy tunes and dance around your kitchen or go outside and chase your dog around. There are lots of easy ways to work exercise into your daily routine; it doesn't have to be something as formal as a trip to the gym!

7. Eat well.

Healthy bodies need good nutrition to function properly and cope with every day stressors. If you're unsure about what types of food are best for you, consider seeing a naturopath or dietician for advice. If you're constantly under a lot of stress, ask if you should be adding a vitamin supplement to your diet, as well.

Also, be sure to keep your energy levels up throughout the day; it's so easy to get caught up in all the "to-do list" task items you've got to get through that you either forget to eat regularly, or you end up grabbing whatever empty-calorie snack item happens to be at hand (chips, cookies, candy... the usual suspects). Make it a point to keep healthy snacks available and at hand to ward off hunger-induced stress attacks.

8. Get some rest.

Getting enough sleep is critical for handling stress. In her book *The Willpower Instinct*, psychologist Kelly McGonigal states that being even "mildly but chronically sleep deprived makes you more susceptible to stress" and decreases your ability to control your emotions and focus your attention.

We all have a tendency to try and cram more into our days at the expense of our sleep time. But constantly reducing the amount of sleep we get results in sleep deprivation and decreased productivity, and it taxes our ability to cope with life.

Chapter 6:
Psychological Stress Busters

"Stress is caused by being HERE
but wanting to be THERE.*"*
~ECKHART TOLLE

Psychological coping strategies involve changes to the ways in which you think about and interpret the events and situations in which you find yourself. Simple changes to your perspective and thought processes can have *huge* effects on your stress levels and experience of life.

1. Use affirmations.

When a negative thought habit becomes ingrained and automatic, you may be causing yourself all sorts of unnecessary stress just because you've formed a habit of expecting to be stressed.

You can counteract negative thought habits by creating and using affirmations, or positive statements that you repeat to yourself in an effort to change an ingrained thought pattern or belief. As you start using affirmations regularly, you will notice yourself becoming naturally more relaxed and at ease.

If you'd like help learning how to create and use affirmations, my book, *The Positive Affirmations Handbook*, will teach you how to create and use effective personal affirmations, and it also provides troubleshooting tips on what to do when your affirmations just aren't working for you.

2. Create a vision board.

A vision board is a powerful tool to help you visualize your life as you want it to be, which in turn helps you to manifest those desires into your reality. A vision board helps you think of what you want as not only possible, but inevitable. And as you begin to believe that something is possible for you, you automatically start taking the actions necessary to make it so.

Likewise, when you don't believe something is possible, you're less likely to even try and make it happen, and more likely to unconsciously take actions that will actually sabotage your own efforts to get what you want. So if you want to become more relaxed and peaceful, create a vision board full of relaxing images and quotes to help you really see and feel yourself as a more relaxed person.

3. Use a personal mantra.

Choose or create a personal mantra, your own special "magic words" that you can whisper to yourself when you feel your stress response kicking in.

Pick a quote or a phrase that reminds you to relax, something that soothes you whenever you hear it and either memorize it or write it down and carry it with you so you can use it whenever you need to.

4. Meditate.

Meditation doesn't have to involve sitting around and chanting "om" while you commune with your higher self (although that actually is a great way to relax!) You can use guided meditations, like the ones that are available on my web site, to help you breathe your tension out, or visualize your way to a calmer state of mind.

If you haven't picked up your free copy of my stress-relief guided meditation yet, you can get it here:

http://www.nathaliethompson.com/stress-relief-meditation .

5. Let go of perfectionism.

Expecting yourself to be perfect at everything you do is the perfect way to set yourself up for excessive stress. If you find that you are constantly criticizing yourself for not being good enough, learn to let it go. Be gentle with yourself and realize that you don't have to be perfect in order to be awesome!

6. Reframe the problem.

Throughout this book, I have reiterated the point that different people can respond to the same situation in different ways, and that one person might find a situation very stressful while another wouldn't be bothered by it at all. A big part of that is perspective, and how the individuals *interpret* the situation they're in.

The next time you find yourself feeling stressed about something, try to look at it from a different perspective. Instead of getting upset over being stuck in a traffic jam, think of it as bonus time for listening to your favourite tunes or audio affirmations. (Plan ahead and keep a CD or USB key in your car!)

7. Look at the big picture.

This is another technique that involves a shift in perspective. Something I've found useful for dealing with stressful situations in my own life is to ask myself if whatever seems to be such a big issue at the moment will actually matter in five years, or even in a month. Just that one little shift in how I look at a situation can make a huge difference in how I react to it.

8. Focus on appreciation.

There's a reason you hear so much about the "attitude of gratitude" lately – it works! Focusing on the things you are grateful for in life, rather than on the things that bother you, has a huge impact on your outlook and experience.

Take some time every day to think of all the things you appreciate in your life, all the things that you are thankful for, and all the things that make you happy. This will instantly reduce your stress levels and shift you to a more positive mood.

Chapter 7:
Environmental Stress
Busters

"DO NOT ANTICIPATE TROUBLE OR WORRY ABOUT WHAT
MAY NEVER HAPPEN. KEEP IN THE SUNLIGHT."
~BENJAMIN FRANKLIN

Environmental coping strategies involve changes to your surroundings; the space in which you actually live and work. You spend all of your time in this world immersed in the space around you, so taking control of that space and making sure it's conducive to the kind of experience you want to have is critical.

1. Unplug.

In today's Digital Age, we are constantly bombarded by information. Any time we turn on the internet, we are subjected to an avalanche of unwanted advertising and headlines we can't avoid, even when we want to.

Between our televisions, radios, cell phones, tablets and laptops most of us are connected all day every day. This 24/7 exposure to endless streams of data that we have to filter and cope with inevitably leads to information overload. It's exhausting. And it's one of the biggest modern-day sources of stress we have.

One of the best things we can do to deal with this is to go "on strike" and unplug completely for at least 24 hours. Turn off all those data sources – every last one of them – for a full day and just take some time to reconnect with your own thoughts. Let yourself slow down, just for one day. But do it regularly... schedule yourself an "off" day at least once a month.

2. Seek the sound of silence.

In modern society, we're almost always surrounded by industrial noises of one sort or another, whether it's ground traffic, airplanes, ventilation systems, other people, or whatever. If you're a noise-sensitive individual, this constant auditory assault that occurs on a daily basis can interrupt your sleep patterns, take a toll on your mental health, and increase your stress level[4]. Finding moments of true silence in which your mind and body can relax and unwind whenever possible is important.

Alternatively, just getting away from the noises of the machine world and enjoying some time immersed in the softer sounds of nature can also be helpful. It's in silence and stillness that we are able to find the moments of peace and clarity that return us to ourselves.

3. Simplify.

One of the biggest areas of stress in many people's lives is clutter. Being surrounded by chaos all the time can really have an impact on your mental health.

Dedicate some time to decluttering your home or office space, and you will likely notice an immediate decrease in your stress levels!

4. Take charge of your schedule.

Overwhelm is a significant source of stress in most people's lives. If you've got too much stuff on your to-do list, perhaps it's time to get clear on what tasks are necessary and what tasks are optional.

Do the important tasks and let the other ones go. Likewise, learn to say no; if you've got enough on your plate as it is, don't agree to take on additional tasks.

5. Do your thing.

Your hobbies and the things that you are interested in are an integral part of who you are, and you need to give yourself permission to express yourself through these means.

When we deny ourselves the pleasure of doing the things we enjoy, it can increase our anxiety and stress levels. Take time to do the things you love most!

6. Protect your relaxation time.

Regularly taking time out to relax is critical to keeping your stress levels under control; even if it's just ten minutes a day to do something like have a quiet cup of tea or chat with a friend.

If you've blocked off a time slot specifically for relaxation and added it to your schedule the same way you add all your other tasks, you're less likely to overlook it or not do it. Protect your "me" time and don't let other tasks or responsibilities encroach on this time.

7. Plan ahead.

Planning ahead and thinking about how long it will take to get somewhere and what you'll need to bring can help you avoid the stress of constantly feeling like you're running late. It can also help you avoid running out the door and forgetting something critical, like a diaper bag or the files for the report you have to present.

8. Engage your senses.

Get creative and try a multi-pronged stress management approach that includes all of your senses. Post images in your office or work space that help you relax, and add some natural elements like a green plant or colourful flowers. Open the window and listen to sounds of nature, or listen to your favourite relaxing music. Make yourself a fragrant cup of tea and close your eyes for a moment while you enjoy the taste, the warmth and the scent. Give yourself permission to just sit back for a spell, put your feet up, enjoy your new space, and let the tension melt away...

Chapter 8:
Social Stress Busters

"I PROMISE YOU NOTHING IS AS CHAOTIC AS IT SEEMS.
NOTHING IS WORTH DIMINISHING YOUR HEALTH.
NOTHING IS WORTH POISONING YOURSELF
INTO STRESS, ANXIETY, AND FEAR."
~STEVE MARABOLI

Social coping strategies are those that involve the other people in your life. While you can't control what other people say or do, you *can* control how *you* interact with them. To a certain extent, you can also control whether or not you are exposed to social situations that you know will trigger your stress response (use your log from Chapter 3 to help you figure out what your particular triggers are).

1. Avoid situations that stress you.

In other words, just don't go there for heaven's sake! You have a lot more control over some of the stressful situations around you than you think and you can choose not to expose yourself to those situations if you want to.

For example, if you get stressed by seeing and hearing things on the radio or the evening news, then turn them off or flip the channel. Make it a point to avoid listening or watching at the times of day where the upsetting stories are most likely to be aired.

2. Avoid negative people.

If there is someone in your life who constantly causes you stress, or upsets you every time you interact with them, stop seeing them. Either minimize the amount of time you have to spend with that person, or just break off the relationship altogether.

This is obviously much harder to do if it's someone you live with or have to interact with on a regular basis so if you're in that situation, try some of the other strategies to help buffer you for the times you do have to be exposed to that person.

3. Avoid hot-button topics.

If talking about certain topics gets you riled up (for example, topics like religion, sports or politics) then stop talking about them. If someone brings one of your hot-button topics up, try steering the conversation in another direction (e.g. "Hey, how's your garden doing this year?").

If you can't redirect the conversation, then politely excuse yourself and go talk to someone else. ("Excuse me for a moment; I just remembered I need to call my dog-walker.")

4. Build your tribe.

Surround yourself with people who uplift and support you; people you are happy to be around. If you are living with people who constantly bring you down and you are not able to change your living situation, then find friends that make you happy. Online friends count, too, so check out blogs and forums dedicated to the things you are interested in and make some connections.

Human beings are social creatures, and we're happiest when we feel like we belong within a group. This does *not* mean you need to change who you are in order to make yourself fit into a group that doesn't feel right to you just so that you're part of a group. It means that you need to find your "people" – the ones you *do* fit with, just the way you are. The ones who will support you when you're down and celebrate with you when things are going well, and the ones for whom you will do the same.

5. Choose Your Cause.

In his book *Flourish*, Dr. Martin Seligman discusses the psychology of human flourishing, and he says that there are five factors that contribute to our well-being. The first three of these factors are: positive emotion, engagement, and meaning. Essentially, finding "something greater" to believe in and dedicate ourselves to helps us to become all that we can be.

Having something in our lives that we derive pleasure from, something that engages us to such an extent that we lose track of time or "lose ourselves" in doing, and something that we ascribe meaning to – all of this helps to keep us happy and well. Finding a greater purpose (whatever than means for you) to pour your time and energy into will help you in all areas of your life.

6. Laugh more.

They say laughter is the best medicine, and it's true. Studies have shown that laughter really does reduce tension and stress[5] so watch a comedy, browse funny pins on Pinterest, give yourself permission to watch those "cats doing crazy things" videos on YouTube, or just ask a little kid to tell you his best knock-knock joke!

If you can find a way to laugh with friends, you'll get an even bigger boost. In *Flourish*, Seligman also says that "other people are the best antidote to the downs of life and the single most reliable up". If you think back through your most cherished memories – the times in your life when you were happiest – I'm willing to bet that most of them involved at least one other person.

7. Shake it up.

Sometimes, you just need a break and a change of perspective to ease your stress. Step out of your usual routine and do something different! Call up some friends and plan to do something this weekend that you've never done before or go somewhere you've never gone before.

Alternatively, go do something new yourself and make it a point to meet new people while you're at it. Push your comfort zones a bit and see what happens. Go rock climbing, sign up for an art class, or volunteer your time in an organization that interests you.

8. Find a furry friend.

Numerous studies have shown that spending time with friendly, furry animals reduces blood pressure and anxiety levels.[6]

If you're fortunate enough to have a pet like a cat or a dog, take a minute or two to just to pet your furry friend. You'll probably both feel better! It's hard to feel stressed with a purring ball of fluff in your lap or a happily wagging tail by your side.

Chapter 9:
What's Next?

"THERE'S GOING TO BE STRESS IN LIFE,
BUT IT'S YOUR CHOICE WHETHER TO
LET IT AFFECT YOU OR NOT."
~ VALERIE BERTINELLI

Finished the book and wondering what to do next? Here is what I suggest: practice the Stress-Buster techniques you've chosen for your action plans. Pick the one that you like best and do it today, at least once.

As mentioned in the introduction, the more often you use the techniques and strategies in this book, the easier they get and the more powerful and effective they become. Your success in ending rampant stress lies in creating new habits of thought and behaviour that will allow you to live your life in a more peaceful and relaxed way, so be sure to deliberately practice the techniques you've chosen for yourself as often as you can.

Once you've gone through the "Four-Step Stress Reduction Process", created your action plan, and tried some of Stress Buster Strategies, do make it a point to download and listen to the free guided meditation for stress relief that is included as a free bonus with the purchase of this book. This audio file has been specifically designed to gently lead you through a directed breathing exercise that will help you reduce stress and relax both your mind and body.

My suggestion is that you use this meditation every night before you go to bed; the relaxed feeling you will get from the meditation may also help you to sleep better! Alternatively, you can use the audio whenever you are feeling particularly tense or anxious (except when driving or doing anything else that requires concentration, obviously), to help you cope with the anxiety and increase your sense of tranquility.

Additionally, if you'd like a daily dose of uplifting stuff to keep you focused on the changes you're trying to make in your life and keep you inspired, I invite you to join the Vibe Shifting community on Facebook.

A Decision to Change

Stress may be a fact of life, but we don't have to let it get the better of us. Constantly allowing ourselves to become frazzled and overwhelmed leads to long term mental and physical health issues that we'd all rather avoid, and it causes us to lose our ability to enjoy all the beauty and pleasure that life has to offer.

Learning to cope with stress involves accepting responsibility for our own lives and our reactions and responses to the events and circumstances therein; it involves reclaiming our power, and making the choice to create positive changes in our thoughts and habits by deliberately choosing to find and use strategies that work for us.

If you've gone through this book, then you now have the tools at hand to guide you through this process of change. But here's the thing about most self-help books: many people buy them, but a lot of those people don't even read them after they've bought them. And out of those people who *do* read them, most of them will never actually use the information provided. Reading about stress-relief strategies is all well and good, but if you don't take action and *use* the processes and techniques in this book, they can't help you, plain and simple.

Remember that all the power to change resides with YOU; no one else can do this for you. So make the decision to make a change and start *doing*. Your stress-free life awaits...

A Letter to the Reader

Dear Reader,

I hope you enjoyed *Simple Strategies for Stress Relief*. Thank you so much for taking time out of your busy schedule to read it!

As you know, reviews are the lifeblood of any book – especially for us indie authors. Without them, our books quickly disappear from book store search algorithms and fade into obscurity. And that makes the books very, very sad.

If you'd like to help make this particular book very, very happy, it would be thrilled if you could leave it a review. You can do that right here:

(Just scan the QR code, and then click the "Write a Customer Review" button at the bottom of the page). Thanks so much, from both me and my book, and have a fantastic day!

Light and love,
Nathalie Thompson

Other Books By
This Author

The Positive Affirmations Handbook
fearLESS
Simple Strategies for Stress Relief

The Life Shifting Series:

Mind Shifting
Soul Shifting (Coming Soon!)

Coloring Books:

Mystical Mantras Coloring Book
Celtic Knots Coloring Book

About the Author

Nathalie Thompson wants to live in a world where coffee pots are never empty and everyone is living the extraordinary life of their dreams.

A transformation catalyst and motivational expert, she is the author of *fearLESS* and *Mind Shifting* and her articles have been featured on the *Huffington Post* and on the blogs of NYT best-selling inspirational authors Pam Grout and Mike Dooley.

Connect with her and start transforming *your* dreams into reality over at www.VibeShifting.com!

/vibeshifting   @vibeshifting

References

[1]

https://www.google.ca/?ion=1&espv=2#q=definition%20of%20stress

[2]

https://www.apa.org/news/press/releases/stress/2014/stress-report.pdf

[3]   http://www.webmd.com/mental-health/effects-of-stress-on-your-body

[4] Nivison, M.E. & Endresen, I.M. J Behav Med (1993) 16: 257. doi:10.1007/BF00844759

[5] http://europepmc.org/abstract/MED/11211708/

[6] http://www.ncbi.nlm.nih.gov/pubmed/19185195

FREE MP3 DOWNLOAD

Don't forget your stress relief guided meditation!

Sign up for the author's Readers Group and get a free MP3 stress relief guided meditation to take what you learn in this book to the next level!

Download your free copy today at:

http://nathaliethompson.com/stress-relief-meditation/

www.ingramcontent.com/pod-product-compliance
Lightning Source LLC
Chambersburg PA
CBHW031611040426
42452CB00006B/476

9780994884497